BIRTHSIGNS
the celtic tree year

D1407906

Molly Gowen and Lavinia Hamer

TOWN HOUSE

Published in 1993 by
Town House and Country House
42 Morehampton Road
Donnybrook
Dublin 4
Ireland

A CIP catalogue record for this book is available from
the British Library.

ISBN: 0-948524-61-8

Managing editor: Treasa Coady
Text editor: Elaine Campion
Book design: Bill Murphy
Printed in Hong Kong

Contents

Preface

I first discovered the Beth-Luis-Nion tree calendar several years ago in Robert Graves's *The White Goddess*. Around the same time I was privileged to meet Lavinia Hamer, who shares with me a Celtic ancestry, an interest in all ancient things and a deep love of the natural world. Within a few days we had decided to undertake this work, which took shape very quickly. From its inception this book, like its companion, *Birthsigns from the Celtic Animal Year* (Town House, 1993), has been a shared project. Working with Vin has been a pleasure, a privilege and an inspiration, and her enchanting artwork speaks for itself.

The purpose of this book is to introduce, or reintroduce, to the world the major deities of the Celtic tradition, a tradition that has as full a range of gods and goddesses as can be found in Greek, Roman and Egyptian mythology. These are presented within the framework of the ancient Celtic tree calendar, a calendar that consisted of thirteen lunar months and one day — the 'year and a day' that is often referred to in folk and fairy tales. Known as the Beth-Luis-Nion, this calendar was in existence long before the Roman calendar that we use today. Each month had its own tree — Beth was the month of the birch, Luis the month of the rowan, Nion the month of the ash, and so forth. The individual months also had their own deities, colours and birds. This calendar of tree magic was part of the religious system of the Celts and has been passed down in an oral tradition that spans three thousand years.

It is important to remember that mythology is not an exact science, and that traditions and beliefs tend to overlap or differ slightly from country to country. There are often similar gods in the different traditions, for example, there is a father god in all traditions but he is known by different names: in the Irish tradition he is Daghdha Mór, lord of the Tuatha De Danann; in the Welsh tradition he is Doged or Diwrnach Maer; and he appears as Zeus, Thor and Jupiter in Greek, Nordic and Roman mythology. I have included a Glossary for further information and elucidation of unfamiliar terms.

I hope this book will bring joy and pleasure to everyone who reads it and that it will inspire them to a further interest in this area.

Finally, I wish to dedicate my work to my paternal grandfather, Gully Gowen, on whose knee I first heard the ancient tales, and to my maternal grandfather, Jack McHenry, who first introduced me, at the age of six or so, to ogham stones, in the cool cloisters of University College Cork. To both of you, in living, loving memory.

Molly Gowen
May 1993

TREE: BIRCH

BIRD: PHEASANT

COLOUR: WHITE

DEITY: OGHMA (worshipped in Europe, Ireland and Wales)

Personal attributes: *ambitious, patient, prudent. Sometimes mean, capricious, pessimistic.*

Oghma speaks:

*Of Instructors I am the
  Highest.
With my Lord I work
  ceaselessly throughout the
  spheres.
The Ark sheltered me until the
  calming of the waters.
I have journeyed through India
  and Asia:
I have reached the ruins of
  Troy.*

*I am Namer of constellations:
I dwell among cherubim who
  worship beyond the summer
  stars.
I watched from the galaxy as
  Rome was built.
Word was mine before I spoke.
My voice breaks the Eternal
  Silence.*

(Adapted from *Hanes Taliesen*,
13th C. Welsh, by M Gowen)

Beth is the month of the birch tree and the first letter of the ogham alphabet, a Goidelic (Gaelic) alphabet that was widely used in pre-Roman Britain and in Ireland. Its bird is the pheasant, its colour white.

The word 'birch' is probably derivative of Sanskrit, *bhurga* meaning 'tree whose bark was used to write upon'. The inner bark of the birch tree has frequently been used as writing material. Legend tells us that the first inscription in Ireland was written on birch bark by Oghma, Sun Face, God of Eloquence. Oghma was the son of Daghdha Mór, king of the Tuatha De Danann. He was known as Ogmias in Gaul and he endures as the holy word 'Om' in contemporary meditation. Oghma was ruler of the Zodiac, president of festivals, founder of cities, healer of the sick and patron of archers and athletes.

The god Oghma in a birch wood.

Ogham stones can be found
in all parts of Ireland. They
are used for obituary and
commemorative purposes,
and for the demarcation of
territorial boundaries.

TREE: ROWAN

BIRD: DUCK

COLOUR: GREY

DEITY: BRÍD (worshipped in Europe, Ireland and Scotland)

Personal attributes: *independent, honest, intellectual. Sometimes aloof, irritable, rebellious.*

The Song of Bríd

Flame red are my berries;
I bring life to earth;
Who cradled the Christ child
The night of his birth.

My mantle the heavens;
With stars am I crowned;
Flood mother, flame daughter
In wisdom profound.

Pure white are my flowers;
Flame red is my fruit;
I burn in the hearth fires
Of Eternal Truth.

I am Bríd of the poets;
I am Bríd of Kildare;
I am Bríd of the wellsprings;
I will always be here.

Bright red are my berries;
Of lightning my flame;
My presence among you,
Saint Bríd is my name.

(M Gowen)

Luis (Goidelic or Gaelic word for 'flame') is the month of the rowan, tree of quickening. Its bird is the duck. Its colour is grey, for grey is the colour of floodwater and rainy skies.

The rowan is also known as witchwood or quickbeam. It is associated with lightning. In ancient times, fires were lit with its wood for many sacred purposes. This suggests perhaps the origin of its name, 'mountain ash'.

The rowan is sacred to Bríd, a deity who forms part of the very ancient triad of Anu, Danu and Brigid. Bríd is the daughter of Bóinn, goddess of the river Boyne, and of Daghdha Mór, king of the Tuatha De Danann. Her consort is Aengus Óg, God of Love.

Bríd's name comes from the Sanskrit *Brizien*, meaning 'to enchant', and her link with the rowan is further expressed in the beautiful title often given to her, 'Flame of the two eternities'.

The Goddess Bríd holding her daughter

'Her vestment was . . . somewhere yellow as the crocus flower, somewhere shining white, somewhere rosy red, somewhere flaming. Her cloak was utterly dark and obscure and throughout its surface the stars glimpsed . . . and the moon in mid-month which shone like a flame of fire.' (From Lucius's vision of the Great Mother in Apuleius's Golden Ass, *2nd C. AD.)*

Bríd is a mother goddess and midwife, protector of women, children and the natural world. Her eyes glitter up from the waters of wells (hence such placenames as Bridewell). She is patron of poetry, smithcraft and healing, similar to Athena or Minerva in the Greek and Roman traditions.

The worship of Bríd has survived in the reverence held by a great many Irish and Scottish people for St Brigid, the wise abbess of Kildare who lived in the sixth century. Many of the legends that surround St Brigid are part of the pre-Christian worship of the goddess Bríd. A rowan branch was hung over the thresholds of houses on St Brigid's Day, the festival of spring or Imbolic.

9

TREE: ASH

BIRD: SNIPE

COLOUR: CLEAR

DEITY: GWYDION (worshipped in Wales)

Personal attributes: *imaginative, sensitive, intuitive. Sometimes neurotic, absent-minded, dependent.*

The Song of Gwydion

I am Gwydion
Shining bright.
I am Gwydion
Snipe in flight.

Know me. Gwydion
Runic bard,
Poet, Father,
Ancient Word.

Old songs, gold songs
True I sing.
Children, children,
Welcoming.

Words on paper,
Sacred, old.
I am Gwydion,
Ash God Gold.

Ash tree, ash tree,
Wind at sea.
I am Gwydion,
Come to me.

(M Gowen)

Nion is the month of the ash, tree of sea power, or the power that resides in water. Its bird is the snipe. Its colour is clear, 'for clear is the colour of the wind'. This is the Mad March Wind 'that whirls like a snipe', spiralling upwards as the poet soars heavenwards towards immortality.

Oars and coracle slats were made from ash wood in Ireland. There were also five sacred ash trees in Irish mythology.

Nion's deity is Gwydion, Ollav poet, father of Welsh imaginative poetry, inventor of runes, patron of language, and a much-loved sacrificial hero. This delightful god is also a magician, skilled in transformation, in miracles. Gwydion corresponds to Odin, the Nordic god of wisdom and poetry and the inventor of runes. Odin's ash tree, named Ygdrasill, is the Tree of Life. The roots of the ash tree have

The creation of Blodeuwedd by Gwydion as a wife for his protégé, Llew Llawgyffes, who could not marry a mortal woman.

'And they took the flowers of the oak tree and the flowers of the broom and the flowers of the meadowsweet and out of these they created the fairest and most perfect girl that man had ever seen and they called her Blodeuwedd.'
(From the Mabinogion)

the same breadth as its branches, denoting balance and the mirroring unity of Heaven and Earth.

TREE: ALDER

BIRD: GULL

COLOUR: CRIMSON

DEITY: BRAN THE BLESSED
(worshipped in Ireland and England)

Personal attributes: *energetic, impulsive, generous. Sometimes egotistic, aggressive, impatient.*

The Song of Bran the Blessed

I am Oracle;
I am tree of fire;
Bran Bendegeit;
I am Love, desire.

I am tree who burns;
I am He who sees;
My voices whisper
Through tops of trees.

I am time no time;
I can never die;
Burn holy wood
On Calvary.

Red Saturn's song;
Her sighing seas;
I sing bright rings
Eternities.

I am Oracle;
I am tree of fire;
Bran Bendegeit;
I am Love, desire.

Fearn is the month of the alder, tree of fire. Its bird is the gull. Its colour is crimson, for 'crimson is the colour of the glain or magical egg which is found in this month and of the alder dye and of the young son struggling through the haze' (Book of Ballymote).

The 'glain' of the druidic mysteries is the Orphic world egg or egg of the year, from which the Easter egg originates. The first being, Phanes (the light), was born at the centre of this egg, which is sometimes depicted with wings.

This month is associated principally with Bran Bendegeit, Bran the Blessed, the alder god, who was a major and complex deity in the Celtic Pantheon, resembling the Greek Orpheus or Cronus. Bran, father of metaphysics, was, like Orpheus, a skilled harpist with a singing voice of great beauty. Both had violent deaths, after which their

The druid Myrddin or Merlin who found the egg in Tintagel in Cornwall. The hatching out of this egg was celebrated each year at the Spring Festival of the Sun.

heads continued to sing and prophesy. Bran, King of Britain, was an oracular deity, who promoted language as the foundation of culture and the endurance of the old beliefs after the main corpus of knowledge had ceased to function in society.

The alder is the tree from which the earliest European houses were built, situated at the edges of lakes. In Catalonia, whistles are made from alder twigs, reinforcing the myth of song. Bran discovered that alder produced the finest charcoal.

In ancient Ireland and Wales, the felling of the alder was punished by the burning of one's house. This tree was most sacred because, when cut, it bled crimson like a human being.

13

TREE: WILLOW

BIRD: HAWK

COLOUR: SILVER

DEITY: ANU (worshipped in Ireland and Scotland)

Personal attributes: *practical, earthy, loyal. Sometimes inward-looking, single-minded, conservative.*

Act I, Scene III

Witch 1
*A sailor's wife had chestnuts in her lap,
And mounch'd, and mounch'd, and mounch'd:
'Give me,' quoth I: —
'Aroint thee, witch!' the rump-fed ronyon cries.
Her husband's to Aleppo gone, master o' the Tiger.
But in a sieve I'll thither sail,
And like a rat without a tail;
I'll do, I'll do, and I'll do.*

Witch 2 *I'll give thee a wind.*

Witch 1 *Th'art kind.*

Witch 3 *And I another.*

Witch 1
*I myself have all the other;
And the very ports they blow.
All the quarters that they know
I' the shipman's card.I'll drain him dry as hay:
Sleep shall neither night or day
Hang upon his penthouse lid;
He shall live a man forbid.
Weary sev'n-nights, nine times nine,
Shall he dwindle, peak, and pine:
Though his bark cannot be lost,
Yet it will be tempest-tost.*

(From *Macbeth* by William Shakespeare)

Saille is the month of the willow, the tree of enchantment. Its bird is the hawk, its colour silver. This is the month of which Amerghin the Druid sang, 'I am a hawk on a cliff.'

The deity of the willow month is Anu, the hag aspect of the Irish triple goddess Anu, Danu and Brigid. She is also Hecate in Shakespeare's *Macbeth*.

In Ireland Anu is also known as the Hag of Beare (an Cailleach Bhéara). She appears as the terrifying Morrigan in the Cú Chulainn sagas. In Wales she is Cerridwen, the moon goddess, and the Old Sow of Menawr Penardd. She is also Morgan le Faye (the fate) in the Grail legends.

As an aspect of Everywoman, this deity has many positive attributes. As Anu she is the high, fruitful mother who turns the wheel of Heaven. Anu, also known as Anan or Innana, is worshipped in Ireland's southern province of Munster as a bringer of plenty,

The Cailleach Bhéara, who was responsible for shipwrecks, sails the ocean in her willow basket.

like Demeter or Rhea in the classical tradition. In Munster also, Aine is a moon goddess in charge of crops and cattle. As a representative of women in the third phase of life, she possesses wisdom, intuition and magical healing powers, as well as strongly established creative links with the natural world.

In her maleficent aspect Anu appears as Black Annis of Leicester, England, a deity who devours children and is responsible for miscarriages. With her sisters, in groups of three or nine, she appears in many myths and legends. She is the wicked witch in all fairy and folk tales.

15

TREE: HAWTHORN

BIRD: NIGHT CROW

COLOUR: LAPIS LAZULI

DEITY: OLWEN (worshipped in Wales)

Personal attributes: *Flexible, subtle, intellectual. Sometimes fickle, unreliable, cunning.*

Sonnet XVIII

*Shall I compare thee to a
    summer's day?
Thou art more lovely and more
    temperate:
Rough winds do shake the darling
    buds of May,
And summer's lease hath all too
    short a date.
Sometime too hot the eye of
    heaven shines,
And often is his gold complexion
    dimm'd;
And every fair from fair some
    time declines,
By chance, or nature's changing
    course, untrimm'd;
But thy eternal summer shall not
    fade,
Nor lose possession of that fair
    thou owest;
Nor shall Death brag thou
    wander'st in his shade,
When in eternal lines to time
    thou growest.
So long as men can breathe, or
    eyes can see,
So long lives this, and this gives
    life to thee.*

(William Shakespeare)

Uath is the month of the hawthorn, tree of cleansing. Its bird is the night crow, its colour lapis lazuli. Amerghin the Druid sang of this month, 'I am fair among flowers.'

In ancient Greece and Rome this was the month when the temples were cleansed and purified in preparation for the mid-summer festival. Uath is associated with maidenhood, innocence and grace.

This is also a dangerous month, however, as strong taboos surround the hawthorn, which must never be disturbed. Such disturbance can lead to the loss of one's children, cattle and money, and other terrible misfortunes. In Wales the hawthorn is the tree of Alphito, the devouring mother, and its branches must never be brought into the house lest she devour the children inside.

There are two very ancient and sacred thorn trees in Britain: the Glastonbury Thorn in England and the Old Bush at St David's in Wales. In the

Olwen, whose hair was yellower than the broom and whose fingers were whiter than wood anemones. Wherever her footprints fell, white trefoil sprang up.

Mabinogion, Great Giant Hawthorn or Ysbaddaden shares the attributes of the Irish Daghdha Mór, king of the Tuatha De Danann. From the union of Ysbaddaden and Alphito was born the beautiful Olwen. She represents the maiden aspect of womanhood, and a similar figure is found in all mythologies. In the Welsh tradition the legend of Culhwch and Olwen describes how the hero wins the beautiful princess. The couple then reign as king and queen of summer.

This exquisite princess is the goddess of innocence and the early morning. She is Primavera, the classical goddess of spring, and Venus, the classical goddess of love, and she possesses the beauty, innocence and grace of the Virgin Mary. She is called 'She of the White Track', which links her to her mother, Alphito, whose milk forms the white track of the Milky Way.

17

TREE: OAK

BIRD: WREN

COLOUR: BLACK

DEITY: DAGHDHA MOR
(worshipped in Ireland and England)

Personal attributes: *refined, individualistic, forward-looking. Sometimes intolerant, arrogant, superficial.*

The Daghdha's Song

I am Daghdha the Mighty,
I am Lord of the Sídhe,
High King of the Druids,
All power lies with me.

I am strength and endurance,
I am wind, I am snow,
I am father progenitor,
From me all things flow.

I am earth, I am water,
I am fire, I am air,
I protect and I nourish,
I have always been there.

I am lightning and thunder,
I am old, I am young,
I am forest and mountain,
I become and become.

I am oak, I am acorn,
I am father and son,
Creator, destroyer,
I have never begun.

(M Gowen)

Duir is the month of the oak, the principal tree of the Beth-Luis-Nion tree calendar. Its bird is the wren, its colour black. The word 'duir' comes from a Sanskrit word meaning 'door'.

In the Book of Ballymote the oak is described thus: 'The oak tree of the Druids is king of the trees. The wren, bird of the Druids and king of the birds, is the soul of the oak.'

The oak is the tree of endurance and triumph. Its deity is Daghdha Mór, lord of the Tuatha De Danann and high king of the gods. This awesome deity appears as Zeus, Thor and Jupiter in Greek, Nordic and Roman mythology.

In Wales Daghdha Mór is called Doged or Diwrnach Maer. He changes the seasons and the weather with his harp, which has the power of human speech, and his inexhaustible cauldron of food and drink makes him the nourishing father of his people. He is the keeper of the fruit trees of plenty and he has two magical

18

The festival of the midsummer solstice. The High God is honoured by the lighting of twin bonfires in the sacred oak grove.

pigs which can be eaten and revived continually.

Daghdha is the strongest of the gods, possessing the greatest druidic magic. He has extraordinary sexual powers. His heavenly consorts include Bóinn and Anu, Eithlenn and Eithnu, and the Morrigan, Queen of Phantoms. Bríd, Ceacht and Porsaibhean (Persephone) are his daughters, while his sons are Aengus Og, Bodhbh Dearg, Lugh (Llew) Lámhfhada, Midhir and Oghma. His other titles are Ruadh Ro-Fheasa (All-Knowing Noble) and Cearas (God of Fire).

The Daghdha is lord of the Sídhe, and can change into twelve distinct avatars. He is associated with the Cerne Abbas giant in Dorset, England, and is said to dwell at the ancient Irish burial site of Newgrange, County Meath, a magical *dún* or fort covered with glistening quartz crystal, which marks the burial place of a mighty Celtic chieftain.

19

TREE: HOLLY

BIRD: STARLING

COLOUR: DARK GREY

DEITY: CÚ CHULAINN (worshipped in Ireland)

Personal attributes: *compassionate, sensitive, impressionable.. Sometimes paranoid, over-cautious, unforgiving.*

Krishna speaks:

Therefore, great warrior, carry on thy fight.

If any man think he slays, and if another thinks he is slain, Neither knows the ways of Truth. The Eternal in man cannot kill, The Eternal in man cannot die.

Weapons cannot hurt the Spirit and Fire can never burn him. Untouched is he by drenching waters, Untouched is he by parching winds.

Beyond the power of sword and fire, Beyond the power of water and winds, The Spirit is everlasting, omnipresent, Never changing, never moving, Ever One.

(*Bhagavad Gita*, Chapter 2, Verses 18–24)

Tinne is the month of the holly, which flowers in July. Its colour is dark grey, the colour of metal. Its bird is the starling.

Amerghin the Druid sang of this month, 'I am a spear that roars for blood.' Tinne is the month of the warrior, whose embodiment in the Irish tradition is Cú Chulainn, the best known and most glorious of the ancient Irish gods and the undefeated champion of Ireland.

Cú Chulainn is believed to have been a deity of the Fir Bolg, a warlike aristocracy which introduced the iron spearhead to Ireland. The Fir Bolg were defeated by the Tuatha De Danann, and now Cú Chulainn endures as a Danann deity. He is a reincarnation of the glorious Llew Lámhfhada who impregnated his mother Deichtire in the form of a mayfly. A solar deity, Cú Chulainn inherited the dazzling brightness of Apollo, the Greek sun-god.

During the battle of Moytirra, between Queen Meadhbh and Cú Chulainn, Queen Meadhbh enlisted the help of the Morrigan, Queen of Phantoms. The Morrigan conjured up demons in the shape of animals to confound Cú Chulainn and his forces. (The crow is her totem bird.)

In Welsh mythology Cú Chulainn's counterpart is the noble Culhwch, cousin of Uther Pendragon, King Arthur's father. Cú Chulainn and Culhwch were similar to Perseus and Aeneas in the classical tradition.

In the English tale of Sir Gawain and the Green Knight, the Green Knight carries a club of holly. Sir Gawain, who represents Christian charity, can be seen as the Christian tradition battling with the Green Man of the Forest.

21

TREE: HAZEL

BIRD: MOORHEN

COLOUR: BROWN

DEITY: FIONN MAC CUMHAILL
(worshipped in Ireland)

Personal attributes: *warm, radiant, strong-willed. Sometimes self-glorifying, indulgent, over-confident.*

The Pool of Knowledge

Unseen by the Gaeil the fountain still springs, feeding the great stream of Fodhla*, and the hazels shed their crimson fruit on the mossy ground and into the clear water, and beneath the ground it sends forth rills feeding the great streams.

But at the time of the shedding of the fruit a salmon, the Eo Feasa, appears in that clear well, and as each divine nut falls upon the surface he darts upwards and devours it.

He is larger and more beautiful than the fishes of his tribe, glittering with crimson stars and bright hues; for the rest of the year he roams the wide ocean and the great streams of Inisfáil*.

* Fodhla = Ireland
* Inisfáil = Ireland

(From *Irish Bardic Poetry* by Standish O'Grady, 1879)

Coll is the month of the hazel, tree of wisdom. Its colour is brown, its bird the moorhen. After the oak, the hazel is the second most important tree in the Beth-Luis-Nion calendar. The felling of either of these trees was punishable by death.

The hazel bears fruit after nine years, and the number nine is sacred to the Muses. This tree brings forth fruit and flowers simultaneously, combining the symbols of beauty and wisdom, as expressed in the name of its deity, Fionn mac Coll (Fair Son of the Hazel) — better known in Ireland as Fionn mac Cumhaill.

Fionn was an early ruler of Ireland who, with his brothers Mac Céacht (Son of the Plough) and Mac Gréine (Son of the Sun), celebrated a marriage with the triple goddess Éire, Fódla and Banba.

Fionn was head of the Fianna, a band of noble warriors. He received the

Fionn mac Cumhaill among the hazel trees at the Pool of Knowledge.

wisdom of Heaven and Earth from the Salmon of Knowledge, the Eo Feasa (see Muin). This salmon was caught by a druid, tutor to Fionn, who instructed Fionn to cook it. As the young Fionn turned the salmon over, he burned his thumb, sucked it and received the gift of knowledge.

In the tribe of King David, Salma is a royal title, hence Solomon. This suggests that the early Christian symbolic fish, Ichthus, was a salmon. This Christian link is beautifully reinforced by the Irish lexicographer Fr Patrick Dinneen, whose dictionary tells us that the Gaelic name for Christ is 'An Coll Cumhra' (Fragrant Hazel).

23

TREE: BLACKBERRY

BIRD: BLUE TIT

COLOUR: GOLD

DEITIES: MEADHBH, FINNTAIN

(worshipped in Ireland)

Personal attributes: *meticulous, helpful, modestly brilliant. Sometimes neurotic, over-critical, perfectionist.*

God speaks:

I am seven battalions (for strength).

I am a flood on a plain (for extent).

I am a wind on the sea (for depth).

I am a ray of the sun (for purity).

I am a bird of prey on a cliff (for cunning).

I am a shrewd navigator (for skill).

I am the gods in the power of transformation (I am a god, a druid, a man who creates magical fire for the destruction of all).

I am a giant with a sharp sword, hewing down an army (for vengence).

I am a salmon in a pool (for swiftness).

I am a skilled artist (for power).

I am a fierce boar (for powers of chieftain-like valour)

I am the roaring of the sea (for terror).

I am a wave of the sea (for might).

(From *The Book of Leacan*)

Muin is the month of the blackberry, from which a heady wine is made. Its bird is the blue tit, its colour gold.

This is the month of the poet, as wine brings visions and poetic inspiration. In ancient times a poet was equal to a queen in status, and was permitted to wear six colours in his robes as queens did.

Queen Meadhbh (Mab) is associated with the blackberry. As a sort of Irish Dionysus, she is the goddess of passion, violence and strong drink. Meadhbh is also an embodiment of the sovereignty of Ireland, for she appointed all the kings of Tara.

In the Christian tradition blackberry juice was believed to be the blood of Christ, probably because it was used as altar wine in the early days. The crown of thorns that Christ wore during his crucifixion was said to be made from its branches.

24

Queen Meadhbh with Finntain the Bard.

Another deity associated with this month is Finntain the Bard, also known as Eo Feasa or the Salmon of Knowledge. Finntain belonged to the race of Cessair, a people wiped out by the Great Flood. He, however, changed into a salmon until the flood subsided, and he reappeared regularly throughout Irish bardic history to provide veracity and continuity to the tradition. He is an embodiment of the spirit of history and antiquity.

25

TREE: IVY

BIRD: MUTE SWAN

COLOUR: BLUE

DEITY: LLEW
(worshipped in Europe, Wales, Ireland and Scotland)

Personal attributes: *generous, peace-making, supportive. Sometimes insensitive, cold, withdrawn.*

The Song of Llew

Llew Llaw is my name, I am light of the sun.
Air, earth and water, belong I to none.
Inhabiting elements, Fire within fire,
Shining in glory, I love and inspire.

I'm centre, I'm circle, sunlight in a flame.
I'm golden, I'm brilliant, and great is my fame.
My sling is the rainbow, the bright stars I wear.
I ride on a bubble, gold shines in my hair.

Even while changing, I still stay the same,
Master magician, Llew Llaw is my name.
Catch me in goldwork and find me in words.
Shining in armoury, jewels and swords.

Inspirer, light bringer and master of dreams.
A moonship; my vessel that changes, it seems.
My faces are many but I am the same,
The Lion of the Long Arm, Llew Llaw is my name.

My light on the green earth turns all into gold.
My power is sacred, my gifts are untold.
In art and in music, in costume I shine,
For I am the God who makes human divine.

(M Gowen)

Gort is the month of the ivy, which grows spirally, symbolising resurrection. Its bird is the mute swan: 'In this month he prepares to follow his companion, the whistling swan' (*Book of Ballymote*). Blue is the colour of this month, 'for blue is the haze on the hill, blue the smoke of the burning weed, and blue the skies before November rain'.

This month's deity is Llew Llaw or Lugh. He is a solar deity, without being the sun itself. He is the magical child of Arianrhod (Silver Wheel), who is also his sister, in the same way as Artemis is

26

The capture of Llew by a moonship. He proceeds to turn the sailors into dolphins, the masts of the ship into snakes, and wreathes everything in ivy. This symbolises the god going through his seasonal changes at the moon's bidding.

sister to Apollo in Greek mythology.

Llew is a pupil to Gwydion, the rune-maker, and they have many adventures. Llew corresponds to the Greek Hermes, God of Revelation, and to the alchemical Mercurius who turns all things to gold. He is the divine intercessor and messenger of the gods. He is the liberator of spirit from matter, master of the creative principle, and the god of enlightenment and civilisation.

In Ireland he is called Lugh Lámhfhada (Lugh the Long-handed). In Wales he is Llew Llawgyffes (Lion of the Long Arm). His feast day is Lughnasa, still celebrated in Ireland on the first Sunday in August.

27

TREE: REED

BIRD: GOOSE

COLOUR: BLUE

DEITY: LIR (worshipped in Scotland and Ireland)

Personal attributes: *passionate, deeply spiritual, enigmatic. Sometimes evasive, superior, over-sensual.*

The Song of Fionnuala

Silent, O Moyle, be the roar of thy water,
Break not ye breezes, your chain of repose,
While murmuring mournfully, Lir's lonely daughter,
Tells to the night star the tale of her woes.

When shall the swan, her deathnote singing,
Sleep, with wings in darkness furled?
When will Heaven, its sweet bells ringing,
Call my spirit from this stormy world?

Sadly, O Moyle, to the winter wave weeping,
Fate bids me languish long ages away.
Yet still in her darkness doth Erin lie sleeping,
Still doth the pure light its dawning delay.

When will that day star, mildly springing,
Warm our isle with peace and love?
When will Heaven, its sweet bell ringing,
Call my spirit to the fields above?

(Thomas Moore, 1779–1852)

Ngetal is the month of the reed, which was harvested at this time of year for the thatching of houses. Its bird is the goose, its colour blue.

Amerghin the Druid sang of this month, 'I am an ominous roar of the sea.' In Ireland the roar of the sea was held to be a prophecy of the death of a king. Set, the Egyptian god of the dead, held a reed sceptre in his hand.

As the reed in water shoots out in a circular formation in all directions, it symbolises the living sun-god, with his myriad of arrows of light. Arrows for hunting were also cut from this plant.

This month's deity is Lir or Lyrr (King Lear), the very ancient sea deity of the Western isles. This deity, son of Daghdha Mór, married Aobh, the daughter of the warrior king Bodhbh Dearg. Aobh bore Lir four children, two sets of twins, but died in her second labour. Later Lir married Aobh's sister Aoife,

The moment of transformation on the sea of Moyle (between Ireland and Scotland).

who became so jealous of her husband's love for the children that, with a magic wand, she turned them into swans. When her father Bodhbh Dearg discovered what she had done, he turned her into the bitter witch of the East Wind. The swans, however, retained their human voices, and during nine hundred years of terrible suffering, continued to sing and make beautiful music. All who heard their songs were healed and comforted in their own sorrow. The swans, Fionnuala, Aodh, Fiachra and Conn, were eventually released from the spell by the hermit St Mochaomhóg, who baptised them before they died in their human form.

29

TREE: ELDER

BIRD: ROOK

COLOUR: RED

DEITY: ARIANRHOD (worshipped in Wales)

Personal attributes: *courageous, innovative, optimistic. Sometimes impatient, irresponsible, fickle.*

The Song of Arianrhod

I am of water, fire and air:
Arianrhod, the ever fair.

Moon maid of diamonds, I
* reside*
Where darkness and the dawn
* divide.*

I tug the waters of the sea:
I'm Muse and Fate and
* Memory.*

My chariot, it climbs the night:
Its pulsing wheels of silver
* light.*

Yes, I am she who shines for all:
In blessed dew and God's
* rainfall.*

Opals, moonstones, crown my
* head:*
I guard and love the Holy Dead.

Enchant, I change and
* rearrange:*
Within my cauldron's pearly
* rim, stars swim.*

I am of water, fire and air:
Arianrhod, the ever fair.

(M Gowen)

Ruis is the month of the elder, tree of the inevitable. Its colour is red, its bird the rook. This is the month when the God of the Year fights the waves of the incoming tide.

Ruis is the last month of the Beth-Luis-Nion tree calendar. The Book of Ballymote tells us 'the rook wears mourning for the year that has died, and blood red are the rags on the elder, a token of the slaughter'.

The elder was said to have been the tree on which Christ was crucified, and on which Judas hung himself.

The concept of Hell did not exist for the Celts, though certain gods ruled the intermediary domain between death and rebirth, the staging post in the Pythagorean-type idea of the transmigration of souls. Midhir the Beautiful in Ireland and Scotland, and Arawn, son of Annwm, in Wales, were such deities, but the figure about whom most

The goddess Arianrhod and her castle in the arms of the whirling North Wind.

information is available is the gentle Arianrhod (Ariadne), also known as Silver Wheel.

A lunar deity, Arianrhod is mother to Llew and sister to Gwydion. The silver-circled daughter of Don (Danu), she presides over a whirling glass castle which lies at the centre or still point of the circling universe, the crown of the North Wind around which the galaxy Corona Borealis revolves. This galaxy is known as 'Caer Arianrhod' or 'the Castle of Arianrhod'.

The wren

The wren is mortally hated by the Irish: for on one occasion when the Irish troops were approaching to attack a portion of Cromwell's army, the wren came and perched on the Irish drums, and by their tapping and noise aroused the English soldiers, who fell on the Irish troops and killed them all. So, ever since, the Irish hunt the wren on St Stephen's Day, and teach their children to run it through with thorns and kill it whenever it can be caught.

A dead wren was also tied to a pole and carried from house to house by (Wren) boys, who demanded money; if nothing was given the wren was buried on the doorstep, which was considered a great insult to the family and a degradation.

(From *Ancient Legends of Ireland* by Lady Wilde, 1888)

This day is usually held to be the day after the winter solstice, the birthday of the Divine Child. It is the day on which Robin Redbreast, as the spirit of the New Year, sets out to kill his predecessor, the Gold Crest Wren, the spirit of the Old Year. The tradition of hunting the wren still survives in Ireland and on the Isle of Man.

Very little is known about this day, which was held to be so sacred that descriptions of associated rituals or festivities do not exist. Amerghin the Druid sang of this day, 'Who but I know the secrets of the unhewn dolmen.' The unnameable day, like the unnameable name of God in the Old Testament, was never pronounced. This suggests a link with the word JWVW, a word that is made up of letters from the Hebrew tetragrammaton, a word that is without vowels and therefore unpronounceable, a symbol of the ineffable mysteries of the gods.

'Who but I know the secrets of the unhewn dolmen.' (Amerghin the Druid)

Mistletoe is associated with this day. As it grows on the oak, it represents the fertility of the oak god, Daghdha Mór (see Duir). It is sacred and mysterious because it is neither shrub nor tree and grows somewhere between Heaven and Earth. Free from definition, it is a symbol of the most sacred mysteries. The cutting of the mistletoe which, legend tells us, took place on this day, signifies the emasculation of the 'old king' by his successor. The Druids also believed that the universe would cease to exist if they did not placate their goddess by sacrifice, fasting and mortification on this day.

33

Glossary

Avatar: The form in which a deity becomes incarnate, for example, man, bull, eagle, etc.

Book of Ballymote: A medieval Irish bardic text.

Druid: Scholar-priest of the Celts.

Fianna: A band of legendary warriors led by Fionn Mac Cumhaill.

Fir Bolg: A legendary race of people who inhabited Ireland before the coming of the Tuatha De Danann.

Fomorians: A race of demons who inhabited the islands around the Irish coast and periodically attacked and laid waste to the island of Ireland. Some of them had only one eye, one arm and one leg. The Fomorians represent the forces of chaos and darkness.

Great Flood (Deluge): Legends of a Great Flood exist in all traditions. The biblical Deluge was substituted by medieval scholars in an effort to reconcile the Judeo-Christian tradition with the older one.

Mabinogion: A title given to four tales in the *Red Book of Hergest*, a fourteenth-century Welsh manuscript. Later extended to the whole collection.

Muses: Goddesses who preside over the arts, especially poetry.

Ogham: An ancient Celtic alphabet of straight lines meeting or crossing the edge of a stone. It is the accepted Irish tradition that this alphabet came from Greece through Spain, and it was widely used in pre-Roman Britain and in Ireland.

Pantheon: Extended family of gods and goddesses pertaining to a particular cultural tradition, for example, Greek pantheon, Celtic pantheon.

Rune: An inscription cut in stone, found in Scandinavia.

Sanskrit: An ancient Indian language used for over three thousand years. All ancient Indian sacred texts were written in Sanskrit, for example, the *Upanisads* and the *Bhagavad Gita*. All contemporary north Indian languages derived from Sanskrit, and many Sanskrit words are to be found in Celtic languages, for example, *skt dwr* becomes *duir* in old Irish and *doras* in modern Irish.

Sídhe: The fairies of Irish folklore. The Sídhe are also said to be either fallen angels or the people of the goddess Danu, the Tuatha De Danann, who went to live underground after they were defeated by the Milesians. The Tuatha De Danann still live under the mountains, rivers and lakes of Ireland, and emerge frequently to hunt, steal babies and beautiful young girls, turn milk sour, and generally confuse and torment people.

Tara: Seat of the ancient High Kings of Ireland, in County Meath. A parliament was held there every three years.

Tetragrammaton: The sacred word in Hebrew that spelt the unnameable name of God. It contains four letters, J H W H (Jahweh).

Tuatha De Danann: *see* Sídhe